★ *Voices from the Civil War* ★

NORTHERNERS

edited by John Dunn

BLACKBIRCH®
PRESS

THOMSON
★
GALE™

San Diego • Detroit • New York • San Francisco • Cleveland
New Haven, Conn. • Waterville, Maine • London • Munich

For more information, contact
The Gale Group, Inc.
27500 Drake Rd.
Farmington Hills, MI 48331-3535
Or you can visit our Internet site at http://www.gale.com

LIBRARY OF CONGRESS CATALOGING-IN-PUBLICATION DATA
Dunn, John M., 1949-
  Northerners / by John M. Dunn.
    p. cm. — (Voices from the Civil War)
Summary: Provides excerpts from letters, books, newspaper articles, speeches, and diary entries which express various views of northern Americans toward slavery and the Civil War.
Includes bibliographical references.
  ISBN 1-56711-791-0 (hardback : alk. paper)
  1. United States—History—Civil War, 1861–1865—Public opinion—Juvenile literature. 2. Public opinion—United States—History—19th century—Juvenile literature. [1. United States—History—Civil War, 1861–1865—Sources. 2. Public opinion—United States—History—19th century. 3. Slavery—History—Sources.] I. Title. II. Series.

E468.9 .D86 2003
973.7—dc21
                                                    2002152786

Printed in United States
10 9 8 7 6 5 4 3 2 1

Contents

LIFE IN THE NORTH

O n the eve of the American Civil War, nearly 30 million people lived in the North. The North ranged from St. Louis, Missouri, to the East Coast, and from the Canadian border southward to Illinois and Pennsylvania.

Two main geographical areas made up the North at this time. They were called the Northwest and the Northeast. The Northeast was America's industrial center. During the 1850s, the states in the Northeast claimed one half of the nation's 140,000 factories. The region was also home to many growing cities, such as New York and Boston. In those cities, European immigrants provided a steady supply of cheap labor for new industries.

Life in the Northwest, meanwhile, was quite different. Much of this region was made up of small farms with farmers who grew wheat and raised cattle, hogs, and sheep. Like its eastern counterpart, the Northwest had several big cities, such as St. Louis, Chicago, and Cincinnati. These urban areas boasted businesses and factories that produced packed meat and farm machinery.

Throughout the North, the land was settled by many different ethnic groups. At the time, most immigrants to the United States arrived in and settled in Northern cities. Big-city newspapers were published in German, Greek, French, and a dozen other languages. Church services were often held in foreign languages. Many city neighborhoods were defined by the immigrants who lived in them.

Immigrants made up a large portion of the population in the American North at the time of the Civil War. This painting shows immigrants' arrival in New York.

This political cartoon warned of the dangers of abolishing slavery.

Though many Northerners were either immigrants themselves or the children of immigrants, they were, for the most part patriotic to the United States. They believed the country was destined to become a great power. Confident in their young nation, Northerners also expected the Union would hold together through any problem great or small.

Despite their faith in the nation, political events that developed during the 1850s worried Northerners. Deep divisions over various issues separated them from their fellow Americans in the South. One of the most divisive issues was that of tariffs, or taxes on imported goods. These taxes made foreign products more expensive. Tariffs gave an advantage to Northern producers who could sell cheaper to Americans. The high tariffs, however, discouraged foreign businessmen from selling to America at all. Without the competition, Northern industries often raised their prices over time. Northern industrialists pressured Congress to keep the tariffs high to protect their businesses. Doing so, however, drove up the costs of goods, especially for Southerners who had to have Northern goods shipped to them.

Another controversial issue that separated North and South was slavery. Most Northerners opposed slavery. Some believed it was immoral. Others thought it served no purpose in a modern society. Many Northern intellectuals, writers, and editorialists publicly condemned Southern slave owners. They opposed any attempts by Congress to allow the expansion of slavery to the newly acquired western territories of the United States, such as Kansas.

Northern opposition to slavery, however, did not mean that most Northerners favored laws giving social or political equality to blacks. Instead, widespread racial prejudice and fear of competing with freed blacks for jobs prompted many white Northerners to oppose citizenship rights for blacks. Segregation (separation) of blacks and whites in public places was also common throughout the North.

Disagreement between the North and the South over slavery underscored another issue that divided the two regions: the role of the central government. For the most part, public opinion in Northern states supported the notion that the federal government in Washington, D.C., was the supreme power. A majority of white Southerners, however, believed that each state government should have absolute control in managing its own affairs. One of the states' rights Southerners claimed was the right of a state to secede or depart from the Union if the citizens believed their interests were being ignored in Washington.

For these reasons, Northerners were divided over how to respond when

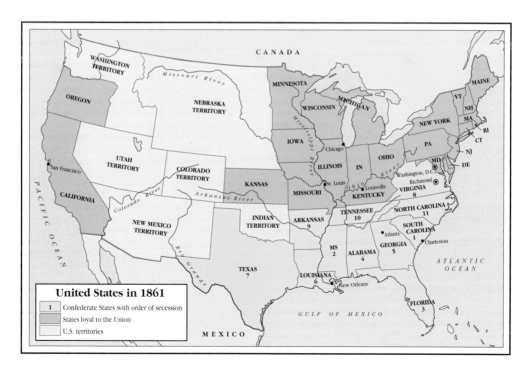

Southern states began to secede from the Union in December 1860. Northerners were further shocked when, in April 1861, Southerners fired on Fort Sumter, a U.S. fort in the harbor of Charleston, South Carolina. Despite this act of rebellion, many Northerners opposed the use of military force to hold the nation together. They argued that a civil war would cause massive harm to the entire nation, and long-lasting bitterness between North and South. Some Northerners also believed that newly elected president Abraham Lincoln lacked the legal authority to use force to stop the South from seceding. Others, however, were angry with the South. They supported Lincoln's argument that the Union should be preserved. They also viewed rebelling Southerners as traitors who had to be stopped by any means.

This split in popular opinion in the North continued throughout the Civil War. Many Northerners supported President Lincoln and his war aims; however, others voiced opposition year after year. By 1864, many Northerners believed the war was going badly for the Union. Some even supported a change in leadership and voted against Lincoln during the presidential campaign in that year. Still others believed Lincoln should seek peace with the South. Lincoln won reelection in 1864, and the tide of the war favored the North despite the critics' beliefs. Union armies eventually bested the South and forced a surrender in 1865.

At the conclusion of the war, Northerners were again divided. This time they disagreed over how the United States should treat the defeated South. Many Northerners, especially Republican members of the U.S. Congress, believed the South should be handled sternly. They wanted the Confederate states to be treated as a conquered nation. Some insisted that Confederate leaders should be executed for treason. Many others, however, agreed with Abraham Lincoln. The president argued that the South had not really ever left the United States. He insisted that the Union should not punish the Southerners who had only been led astray by their slave-owning leaders. Lincoln hoped to rebuild the nation with "charity for all" and "malice towards none."

In April 1865, Lincoln was killed by Southerner John Wilkes Booth. Instead of leniency, a vengeful Congress managed to impose a harsh plan of reconstruction on the South. The Southern states were forced to live under military rule. By imposing such measures, the government drove another wedge between the North and South that lasted for many decades.

Most of the issues that initially separated the North and South were settled during the war. Northern armies preserved the Union and ended slavery. These armies also made clear that the federal government, not the states, would prevail as the dominant voice of government in the United States.

Abraham Lincoln was a controversial president because he challenged the beliefs of Northerners as well as Southerners.

★ *Chronology of the Civil War* ★

November 1860

Abraham Lincoln is elected president of the United States.

December 1860–March 1861

• Concerned about Lincoln's policy against slavery in the West, the South Carolina legislature unanimously votes to secede from the United States. Alabama, Florida, Georgia, Louisiana, Mississippi, and Texas secede from the Union, and form the Confederate States of America.

• Mississippi senator Jefferson Davis becomes president of the Confederacy.

• Arkansas, North Carolina, Tennessee, and Virginia later join the rebellion.

April 1861

Confederate troops fire on Union-occupied Fort Sumter in South Carolina and force a surrender. This hostile act begins the Civil War.

September 1862–January 1863

• Lee's Army of Northern Virginia and George McClellan's Army of the Potomac fight the war's bloodiest one-day battle at Antietam, Maryland. Though the battle is a draw, Lee's forces retreat to Virginia.

• Abraham Lincoln issues the Emancipation Proclamation that declares all slaves in Confederate states to be forever free. Three months later it takes effect.

September 1864

Atlanta, Georgia, surrenders to Union general William T. Sherman, who orders Atlanta evacuated and then burned. Over the coming months, he begins his March to the Sea to Savannah. His troops destroy an estimated $100 million worth of civilian property in an attempt to cut rebel supply lines and reduce morale.

Jefferson Davis, president of the Confederate States of America

July 1861

Confederate troops defeat Union forces at the First Battle of Manassas (First Bull Run) in Fairfax County, Virginia, the first large-scale battle of the war.

April 1862

• Confederate troops are defeated at the Battle of Shiloh in Tennessee. An estimated 23,750 soldiers are killed, wounded, or missing, more than in all previous American wars combined.

• Slavery is officially abolished in the District of Columbia; the only Union slave states left are Delaware, Kentucky, Maryland, and Missouri.

June 1862

General Robert E. Lee assumes command of the Conferate Army of Northern Virginia.

Robert E. Lee

August 1862

Confederate troops defeat Union forces at the Second Battle of Manassas (Second Bull Run) in Prince William County, Virginia.

July 1863

Union forces stop the South's invasion of the North at Gettysburg, Pennsylvania. Lasting three days, it is the bloodiest battle of the war.

November 1863

President Abraham Lincoln delivers the Gettysburg Address in honor of those who died at the war's bloodiest battle at Gettysburg.

April 1865

• Confederate general Robert E. Lee surrenders to Union general Ulysses S. Grant. This ends the Civil War on April 9.

• Five days later, President Lincoln is assassinated by actor John Wilkes Booth.

December 1865

The Thirteenth Amendment becomes law and abolishes slavery in the United States.

Abraham Lincoln,
president of the United States of America

★ *William Lloyd Garrison* ★
LET THE UNION BE BROKEN

Disagreement over slavery divided Northerners and Southerners before the Civil War. Though the practice had been in existence in America for hundreds of years, slavery had almost vanished in the North by the 1850s. In the South, though, as many as 4 million blacks still worked on Southern farms. Abolitionists believed slavery was immoral, if not evil, and they wanted the practice to be outlawed. Among the most controversial abolition- ists was William Lloyd Garrison, editor of a fiery pamphlet called the Liberator. *In the fol- lowing excerpt from a speech delivered on December 2, 1859, Garrison criticizes slavery and slave owners and insists that the North would be better off if the South left the Union.*

• **William Lloyd Garrison, "Tribute to John Brown," December 2, 1859.**

We are living under an awful despotism—that of a brutal slave oligarchy. And they threaten to leave us if we do not continue to do their evil work, as we have hitherto done it, and go down in the dust before them!

Would to heaven they would go! It would only be the paupers clearing out from the town, would it not? But, no, they do not mean to go; they mean to cling to you, and they mean to subdue you. But will you be subdued?

I tell you our work is the dissolution of this slavery-cursed Union, if we would have a fragment of our liberties left to us! Surely between freemen, who believe in exact jus- tice and impartial liberty, and slaveholders, who are for cleaning down all human rights at a blow, it is not possible there should be any Union whatever. "How can two walk together except they be agreed?"

GLOSSARY

• **despotism:** govern- ment led by a ruler with absolute power
• **oligarchy:** govern- ment by a select few
• **hitherto:** until now
• **paupers:** beggars
• **subdue:** overpower
• **dissolution:** breakup
• **compact:** agreement
• **scourges:** whips
• **vital:** necessary

The slaveholder with his hands dripping in blood—will I make a compact with him? The man who plunders cradles—will I say to him, "Brother, let us walk together in unity?" The man who, to gratify his lust or his anger, scourges woman with the lash till the soil is red with her blood—will I say to him: "Give me your hand; let us form a glorious Union?" No, never—never! There can be no union between us. . . .

By the dissolution of the Union we shall give the finishing blow to the slave system; and then God will make it possible for us to form a true, vital, enduring, all-embracing Union, from the Atlantic to the Pacific—one God to be worshipped, one Saviour to be revered, one policy to be carried out—freedom everywhere to all the people, without regard to complexion or race—and the blessing of God resting upon us all!

★ Lyman Trumbull ★
ON THE EVE OF DISUNION

During his political career, Lyman Trumbull served as a state lawmaker, a state supreme court justice, and a U.S. senator. As a U.S. senator, Trumbull was a strong supporter of the Union cause. Trumbull wrote the following letter to a colleague on December 28, 1860. In it, he discusses the likelihood that several Southern states will carry out their threat to secede from, or leave, the Union. His comments concerning President James Buchanan reflect a widely shared distrust of the president. Even though Buchanan publicly declared that he was opposed to Southern secession, he also insisted he was powerless to prevent it. This, according to Trumbull, was the act of a traitor. Trumbull puts more faith in newly elected president, Abraham Lincoln.

• Lyman Trumbull, Letter to O.M. Hatch, December 28, 1860.

Hon. O.M. Hatch

Mr. Buchanan I fear is a Traitor. He seems to be imbecile, weak and wicked. The House [of Representatives] will probably prefer articles of impeachment if he orders Fort [Sumter] surrendered up but I suppose the Senate would not convict. Great efforts are being made to get all the slave states to join in this secession movement. Do not believe they can succeed in this, but if they should between this & the 4th of March [Lincoln's inauguration day], it would be a formidable affair. Nothing is to be made by concessions. . . . Nothing short of surrendering up the Government to the South will satisfy the cotton states. Rule or ruin is their motto. I have all along thought that the leaders of the South outside of the Gulf States only wanted some decent excuse to back down from their position; but the trouble now is leaders no longer control the movement. The rabble have taken it out of their hands. I still think some way will be devised of keeping the border slave states quiet, & in the end the cotton states which secede will be glad to get back. I hope Mr. Lincoln will keep quiet, cool & self possessed, let what will happen. He can not speak to do any good until the 4th of March, & then I trust it will be with a voice which will command obedience. Truly Yours, Lyman Trumbull

GLOSSARY

- **imbecile:** foolish
- **impeachment:** a political process that bring charges of wrongdoing against a public official
- **Fort Sumter:** a Union fort in the harbor of Charleston, South Carolina. After South Carolina seceded from the Union, it demanded that the federal post be surrendered to the state. In April 1861, South Carolina troops fired on the fort and forced its surrender. These were the first shots of the Civil War.
- **formidable:** frightful
- **rabble:** mob
- **border slave states:** pro-slavery states like Kentucky and Maryland that lay between the North and the Deep South.

★ *David Hunter Strother* ★

JOHN BROWN'S EXECUTION

Americans killed one another over slavery for many years before the outbreak of the Civil War in 1861. One of the leading supporters of armed rebellion against slavery was John Brown. He believed that God had elected him to seek revenge against slaveholders. In 1855, in Kansas, Brown and his sons murdered five settlers whom they suspected of being proslavery. Immediately, the killers went into hiding. Brown emerged again on October 16, 1859, when he and a group of eighteen men took hostages and occupied a federal building in Harpers Ferry, Virginia. Brown and his followers hoped to capture weapons stored there and give them to slaves. Fighting soon broke out between Brown's men and a unit of U.S. Marines. Finally, after many of Brown's men were killed or wounded, Brown was captured. Later convicted of inciting a slave uprising, Brown was executed on December 2, 1859. David Hunter Strother, a correspondent for Harper's Weekly *newspaper, witnessed Brown's execution. His account of that event is excerpted here.*

- **David Hunter Strother, "Account of the Execution of John Brown,"** *Harper's* **Weekly, December 1859.**

GLOSSARY

- **waggon:** wagon
- **after part:** rear section
- **dilapidated:** shabby, broken-down
- **particoloured:** showing different colors or tints
- **gibbet:** gallows, a post for hanging criminals
- **solemnity:** seriousness
- **ludicrous:** ridiculous
- **pinioned:** restrained, bound
- **alacrity:** quickness
- **halter:** noose
- **accordingly:** thus

He [Brown] was seated in a furniture waggon on his coffin with his arms tied down above the elbows, leaving the forearms free. The drivers with two others occupied the front seat while the jailer sat in the after part of the waggon. I stood with a group of half a dozen gentlemen near the steps of the scaffold when the prisoner was driven up. He wore the same seedy and dilapidated dress that he had at Harper's Ferry and during his trial, but his rough boots had given place to a pair of particoloured slippers and he wore a low crowned broad brimmed hat (the first time I had ever seen him with a hat). He had entirely recovered from his wounds and looked decidedly better & stronger than when I last saw him. As he neared the gibbet his face wore a grim & grisly smirk which, but for the solemnity of the occasion, might have suggested ideas of the ludicrous. He stepped from the waggon with surprising agility and walked hastily toward the scaffold pausing a moment as he passed our group to wave his pinioned arm & bid us good morning. . . . He mounted the steps of the scaffold with the same alacrity and there as if by previous arrangement, he immediately took off his hat and offered his neck for the halter which was as promptly adjusted by Mr. Avis the jailer. A white muslin cap or hood was then drawn over his face and the Sheriff not remembering that his eyes were covered requested him to advance to the platform. The prisoner replied in his usual tone, "You will have to guide me there."

The breeze disturbing the arrangement of the hood the Sheriff asked his assistant for a pin. Brown raised his hand and directed him to the collar of his coat where several old pins were quilted in. The Sheriff took the pin and completed his work.

He was accordingly led forward to the drop, the halter hooked to the beam, and the officers supposing that the execution was to follow immediately took leave of him. In doing so, the Sheriff enquired if he did not want a handkerchief to throw as a signal to cut the drop. Brown replied, "No, I don't care; I don't want you to keep me waiting unnecessarily."

These were his last words, spoken with that sharp nasal twang peculiar

John Brown (kneeling, right) and his followers occupied the federal building at Harpers Ferry, Virginia, in 1859.

to him, but spoken quietly & civilly, without impatience or the slightest apparent emotion. In this position he stood for five minutes or more, while the troops that composed the escort were wheeling into the positions assigned them. I stood within a few paces of him and watched narrowly during these trying moments to see if there was any indication of his giving way. I detected nothing of the sort. He had stiffened himself for the drop and waited motionless 'till it came.

★ *Culvert Comstock and William Cassidy* ★

CONQUERING THE SOUTH MAY NOT PRESERVE THE UNION

As the nation moved closer to civil war, Northerners disagreed over what to do about the crisis. Some believed the Southern states had the right to secede. Others, however, disagreed. Some who opposed secession favored using military force to keep the South from leaving the Union. This suggestion, however, worried many Northerners who feared that military action would lead to many deaths. They were also concerned that a war would cause bitterness and hatred between the North and South after the fighting stopped. These concerns are evident in the following excerpt of a January 12, 1861, editorial in the Albany, New York, newspaper, the Atlas and Argus. *The editorialist advises the nation to "bid a sad farewell" to the slave states, rather than risk the "terrors and horrors" that would be required to make the South remain loyal to the Union.*

- **Culvert Comstock and William Cassidy, editorial, *Albany Atlas and Argus*, January 12, 1861.**

The sectional doctrines of the Republican party have—as thinking men have foreseen—at last brought us to the verge of civil war. Indeed, war has already commenced. Four States have formally separated from the [Union] and declared themselves independent of the Federal Union and are in the attitude of supporting their position by arms. The Republican leaders adhere to their partisan and sectional dogmas and utterly refuse to do anything to arrest this impending danger and restore peace to the country. The present Congress will do nothing and before its term expires on the 4th of March, thirteen or fourteen of the slave States will have established a separate government, which they will sustain at the hazard of fortune and life. We shall be confronted with the stern issue of peaceable, voluntary separation, or of civil war. We shall be compelled to bid a sad farewell to the brethren with whom we have so long dwelt in liberty and happiness and divide with them the inheritance of our fathers—or to undertake, by all the terrors and horrors of war, to compel them to continue in union with us. We must separate from them peaceably, and each seek happiness and prosperity in our own way—or we must conquer them and hold them as subjugated provinces. Fellow citizens, of all parties and of whatever past views, which course do you prefer? Shall it be peaceable separation or civil war?

If such be the issue—and none can now deny it—before choosing war, it will be well to reflect whether it will effect the desired object of preserving the Union of these States? With thirteen or fourteen States banded together and fighting with as much pertinacity, as our fathers of the Thirteen Colonies, for what *they* deemed their rights and liberties, the war must be a deadly and protracted one. We do not doubt that the

This political cartoon reflected the belief of many Northerners that military action was necessary to battle secession.

superior numbers and resources of the Northern States might prevail. We might defeat them in battle, overrun their country, and capture and sack and burn their cities, and carry terror and desolation, by fire and sword, over their several States. We might ruin the commerce and industry of the country, North and South, sweep the whole land with the besom of war, and cause the nation to resound with the groans of widows and orphans; all this we might do, and through it all, possibly, be able to boast of the triumph of the Federal arms, and to see the stars and stripes wave over every battle field and every smoking city.

But would peace thereby be restored? Would the Union be thus preserved?

LINCOLN DEFENDS HIS CONDUCT

During Abraham Lincoln's time in office, he was one of the most controversial U.S. presidents in history. Because of his strong antislavery views, his election to the presidency in 1860 enraged millions of Southerners. When his presidential victory was secure, one Southern state after another left the Union. During the Civil War, many Northerners also became unhappy with Lincoln. Some thought the war was unnecessary and believed the Union should not stand in the way of Southern secession. Others believed Lincoln was not bold and aggressive enough during the early years of the war. New York Tribune editor Horace Greeley was an outspoken critic. In an editorial on August 19, 1862, Greeley questioned Lincoln's handling of the war. He also criticized the president for not enforcing the Confiscation Act. This newly revised law allowed the president to free slaves who were under the control of the Union military. Greeley further complained that too many escaped slaves who fled to Union troops were being sent away by military commanders. Greeley's words prompted a response from Lincoln. In the following excerpt from Lincoln's reply in July 1862, the president says that his main concern is to save the Union, even if this means not freeing any slaves.

• Abraham Lincoln, in Frank Moore, ed., *The Rebellion Record*, Supplement, vol. I, New York: Putnam, 1866.

Dear Sir:

I have just read yours of the 19th, addressed to myself through the *New York Tribune*. If there be in it any statements or assumptions of fact which I may know to be erroneous, I do not now and here controvert them. If there be in it any

---

Horace Greeley was the outspoken editor of the *New York Tribune*.

inferences which I may believe to be falsely drawn, I do not now and here argue against them. If there be perceptible in it an impatient and dictatorial tone, I waive it in deference to an old friend, whose heart I have always supposed to be right.

As to the policy I "seem to be pursuing," as you say, I have not meant to leave anyone in doubt.

I would save the Union. I would save it the shortest way under the Constitution. The sooner the national authority can be restored, the nearer the Union will be "the Union as it was." If there be those who would not save the Union unless they could at the same time *save* slavery, I do not agree with them. If there be those who would not save the Union unless they could at the same time *destroy* slavery, I do not agree with them. My paramount object in this struggle *is* to save the Union, and is *not* either to save or destroy slavery. If I could save the Union without freeing *any* slave, I would do it; and if I could save it by freeing *all* the slaves, I would do it; and if I could do it by freeing some and leaving others alone, I would also do that.

What I do about slavery and the colored race I do because I believe it helps to save this Union; and what I forbear I forbear because I do *not* believe it would help to save the Union. I shall do *less* whenever I shall believe what I am doing hurts the cause, and I shall do *more* whenever I shall believe doing more will help the cause. I shall try to correct errors when shown to be errors; and I shall adopt new views so fast as they shall appear to be true views.

I have here stated my purpose according to my view of *official* duty, and I intend no modification of my oft-expressed *personal* wish that all men, everywhere, could be free.

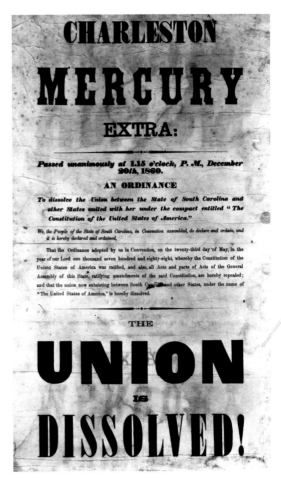

The front page of the *Charleston Mercury*, a South Carolina newspaper, announced that state's secession from the Union on December 20, 1860. South Carolina was the first state to secede.

GLOSSARY

- **erroneous:** incorrect
- **controvert:** dispute
- **perceptible:** apparent
- **dictatorial:** authoritative
- **waive:** dismiss
- **deference:** honor, as a courtesy
- **paramount:** most important
- **forbear:** keep from doing
- **modification:** change

★ S. H. M. Byers ★
PATRIOTIC PRESSURE TO ENLIST

Most Northerners were angry when they received word of the Confederate attack on Fort Sumter, in the harbor of Charleston, South Carolina, on April 12, 1861. Soon, other emotions emerged. War fever and feelings of patriotism swept the villages, towns, and cities of the North. Calls went out across the North for men of all ages to enlist in the Union army and help put down the rebellion. To promote enlistments, town officials set up patriotic mass meetings. Backed by bands playing spirited music, patriotic speakers urged men to enlist. S.H.M. Byers was one of the young men who attended a town meeting in his village of Newton, Iowa.

• **S.H.M. Byers,** *With Fire and Sword.* **New York: Neale, 1911.**

I t all came about through a confusion of names. . . . Everybody was there, and everybody was excited, for the war tocsin was sounding all over the country. A new regiment had been ordered by the governor, and no town was so quick in responding to the call as the village of Newton. We would be the very first. Drums were beating at the mass-meeting, fifes screaming, people shouting. There was a little pause in the patriotic noise, and then someone called out, "Myers to the platform!" "Myers! Myers! Myers!" echoed a hundred other voices. Mr. Myers never stirred, as he was no public speaker. I sat beside him near the aisle. Again the voices shouted "Myers! Myers!" Myers turned to me, laughed, and said, "They are calling you, Byers," and fairly pushed me out into the aisle. A handful of the audience seeing Myers would not respond, did then call my own name, and both names were cried together. Some of the audience becoming confused called loudly for me. "Go on," said Myers, half-rising and pushing me toward the platform.

I was young—just twenty-two—ambitious . . . and now was all on fire with the newly awakened patriotism. I went up to the platform and stood by the big drum. The American flag, the flag that had been fired on by the South, was hanging over my head. In a few minutes I was full of the mental champagne that comes from a cheering multitude. I was burning with excitement, with patriotism, enthusiasm, pride, and my enthusiasm lent power to the words I uttered. I don't know why nor how, but I was moving my audience. The war was not begun to put down slavery, but what in the beginning had been an incident I felt in the end would become a cause.

GLOSSARY

- **tocsin:** alarm
- **mental champagne:** giddy feeling, as if he had drunk champagne
- **multitude:** crowd
- **flogged:** whipped
- **overseer:** a supervisor of slaves
- **perpetuate:** continue

The Confederate attack on Fort Sumter on April 12, 1861, marked the start of the Civil War.

The year before I had been for many months on a plantation in Mississippi, and there with my own eyes had seen the horrors of slavery. I had seen human beings flogged; men and women bleeding from an overseer's lash. Now in my excitement I pictured it all. I recalled everything. "And the war, they tell us," I cried, "is to perpetuate this curse!" In ten minutes after my stormy words one hundred youths and men, myself the first, had stepped up to the paper lying on the big drum and had put down our names for the war.

★ *Frederick Douglass* ★

FREDERICK DOUGLASS SUPPORTS LINCOLN'S ANTISLAVERY POLICY

On September 22, 1862, President Abraham Lincoln issued the Emancipation Proclamation. The proclamation granted freedom to all slaves who lived in states rebelling against the U.S. government. The proclamation officially made the Civil War a fight against slavery. As soon as Lincoln issued it, the Emancipation Proclamation drew criticism from both the North and South. Southern slave owners refused to let their slaves go. They argued that the president had no legal authority to grant slaves freedom. Critics in the North, meanwhile, argued that the president's proclamation had been slow in coming and did not go far enough. Frederick Douglass, an escaped slave living in the North who became a well-known author and lecturer, was optimistic about the proclamation. Though Douglass argued that Lincoln had been too slow in helping blacks obtain freedom, he was also convinced that Lincoln was sincere in his efforts to end slavery. Douglass expressed these views in an article from the October 1862 issue of his newspaper, Douglass' Monthly.

● **Frederick Douglass, editorial, *Douglass' Monthly*, October 1862.**

O pinions will widely differ as to the practical effect of this measure [the Emancipation Proclamation] upon the war. All that class at the North who have not lost their affection for slavery will regard the measure as the very worst that could be devised, and as likely to lead to endless mischief. All their plans for the future have been projected with a view to a reconstruction of the American Government upon the basis of compromise between slaveholding and non-slaveholding States. The thought of a country unified in sentiments, objects and ideas, has not entered into their political calculations, and hence this newly declared policy of the Government, which contemplates one glorious homogeneous people, doing away at a blow with the whole class of compromisers and corrupters, will meet their stern opposition. Will that opposition prevail? Will it lead the President to reconsider and retract? Not a word of it. Abraham Lincoln may be slow, Abraham Lincoln may desire peace even at the price of leaving our terrible national sore untouched, to fester on for generations, but Abraham Lincoln is not the man to reconsider, retract and contradict words and purposes solemnly proclaimed over his official signature. . . .

GLOSSARY

- **homogeneous:** of the same composition
- **corrupters:** spoilers
- **prevail:** win
- **retract:** take back [the proclamation]
- **fester:** decay
- **diminishing:** reducing
- **contend:** deal with
- **confide:** trust

This painting shows Abraham Lincoln at work on the Emancipation Proclamation, the document that freed the slaves.

To look back now would only load him with heavier evils, while diminishing his ability, for overcoming those with which he now has to contend. To recall his proclamation would only increase rebel pride, rebel sense of power and would be hailed as a direct admission of weakness on the part of the Federal Government, while it would cause heaviness of heart and depression of national enthusiasm all over the loyal North and West. No, Abraham Lincoln will take no step backward. His word has gone out over the country and the world, giving joy and gladness to the friends of freedom and progress wherever those words are read, and he will stand by them, and carry them out to the letter. If he has taught us to confide in nothing else, he has taught us to confide in his word.

Frederick Douglass, a well-known author and speaker, was an escaped slave from the South.

★ *New York Times* ★
THE NEW YORK DRAFT RIOTS

By the summer of 1863, the Union army needed more men to fill its ranks. This caused President Abraham Lincoln to issue a federal draft. The draft provoked hostile reactions in many Northern cities. Among the angriest Northerners were the poor working-class Irish immigrants in New York City. Already resentful that they had to compete with blacks in the North for low-wage jobs, many of these immigrants saw no reason to fight or die on behalf of blacks in the South. When the names of the first draftees were announced on July 11, 1863, mobs of mostly Irish immigrants in New York City exploded with rage. They rioted for three days, burned buildings, and killed bystanders. Mobs also lynched blacks and burned a black orphanage. Order was not restored until the fourth day of rioting when federal troops entered the city and quelled the disturbance. The following excerpt is from a July 14, 1863, New York Times article. In it, the author describes how one disturbance broke out in front of a U.S. Army facility in downtown New York.

GLOSSARY

- **foundries:** factories
- **compelled:** forced
- **formidable:** large and frightful
- **irruption:** a violent rush
- **blank cartridges:** empty, harmless shells
- **demoralized:** robbed of the will to fight
- **implements:** tools
- **refuge:** haven, shelter
- **thither:** there
- **marauding:** robbing
- **infuriated:** angry
- **intoxicated:** drunk
- **thronged:** crowded
- **instigated:** urged

• **Article on New York Draft Riots, *New York Times*, July 14, 1863.**

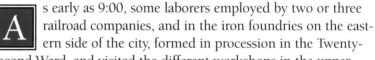

As early as 9:00, some laborers employed by two or three railroad companies, and in the iron foundries on the eastern side of the city, formed in procession in the Twenty-second Ward, and visited the different workshops in the upper wards, where large numbers were employed, and compelled them, by threats in some instances, to cease their work. As the crowd [grew], their shouts and disorderly demonstrations became more formidable. . . . Scarcely had two dozen names been called [by the drafting officers], when a crowd, numbering perhaps 500, suddenly made an irruption in front of the building, attacking it with clubs, stones, bricks, and other missiles. . . . Following these missiles, the mob rushed furiously into the office on the first floor, where the draft was going on, seizing the books, papers, records, lists, [etc.] all of which they destroyed. . . . The drafting officers were set upon with stones and clubs, and, with the reporters for the Press and others, had to make a hasty exit through the rear. . . .

[Soldiers came to stop the riot.]

Facing the rioters, the [soldiers] were ordered to fire, which many of them did, the shots being blank cartridges, but the smoke had scarce cleared away when the company (which did not num-

PROVOST GUARD ATTACKING THE RIOTER'S

After four days of mayhem, federal troops fired on a mob of rioters angered by the federal draft.

ber more than fifty men, if as many) were attacked and completely demoralized by the mob, who were armed with clubs, sticks, swords, and other implements. The soldiers had their bayonets taken away, and they themselves were compelled to seek refuge in the side streets, but in attempting to flee thither, several, it is said, were killed, while those that escaped, did so only to be hunted like dogs. . . . They were chased by the mob, who divided themselves into squads, and frequently a single soldier would be caught in a side street . . . and the poor fellow would be beaten almost to death.

Elated with success, the mob, which by this time had been largely reinforced, next formed themselves into marauding parties, and paraded through the neighboring streets, looking more like so many infuriated demons, the men being more or less intoxicated, dirty and half clothed. . . . The streets were thronged with women and children, many of whom instigated the men to further work of blood.

★ Richard Cordley ★

MASS MURDER IN KANSAS

Some of the most brutal killings during the Civil War took place along the border of Missouri and Kansas, where proslavery and antislavery settlers lived side by side. Small groups of armed civilians on both sides waged murderous attacks on settlers who gave food and supplies to Union or Confederate soldiers. One of these attacks came on August 21, 1863, when a band of 450 men, including outlaws, led by William Clark Quantrill attacked the antislavery town of Lawrence, Kansas. The raiders murdered at least 150 men and then burned and looted the town. One of the survivors was a minister named Richard Cordley. He escaped the attack with his wife and child. When the killers left, Cordley returned to Lawrence and wrote this account of the massacre.

- **Richard Cordley, *A History of Lawrence, Kansas: From the Earliest Settlement to the Close of the Rebellion.* Lawrence, KS: E.F. Caldwell, 1895.**

GLOSSARY

- **ransacked:** searched through
- **charred:** scorched
- **consumed:** destroyed, burned up
- **oppressive:** overpowering
- **undermost:** lowest
- **fondling:** handling fondly
- **piteously:** sadly
- **wailing:** long, intense crying
- **lamentations:** cries of sadness or mourning
- **exertions:** forceful actions or efforts
- **salutation:** greeting

The buildings on Massachusetts street were all burned except one, and that had been ransacked and robbed, and two boys lay dead upon the floor. The fires were still glowing in the cellars. The brick and stone walls were still standing bare and blackened. The cellars between looked like great caverns with furnaces glowing in the depths. The dead lay all along the street, some of them so charred that they could not be recognized, and could scarcely be taken up. Here and there among the embers could be seen the bones of those who had perished in the buildings and been consumed where they fell. . . . The sickening odor of burning flesh was oppressive. . . . Around one corner lay seventeen bodies. Back of a livery stable on Henry street lay five bodies piled in a heap. The undermost man of these was alive, and had lain under the dead for four hours, and so saved himself from a fatal shot. He was severely wounded but recovered. Going over the town [I] saw the dead everywhere, on the sidewalks, in the streets, among the weeds in the gardens, and in the few remaining homes. The women were going about carrying water to the wounded, and covering the dead with sheets. . . . Now and then [I] came across a group, a mother and her children watching their dead besides the ashes of their home. A little later there could be seen a woman sitting among the ashes of a building holding in her

The antislavery town of Lawrence, Kansas, was attacked and looted by proslavery settlers in the 1863 Quantrill raid.

hands a blackened skull, fondling it and kissing it, and crying piteously over it. It was the skull of her husband, who was burned with the building. But there was not much weeping and not much wailing. It was too deep and serious for tears or lamentations. All addressed themselves to the sad work that had to be done.

No one realized the extent of the disaster until it was over. Every man was so isolated by the presence of the raiders in every part of the town, that each knew only what he saw. . . . Besides the buildings on the business street, about one hundred houses had been burned, and probably as many more had been set on fire and saved by the heroic exertions of the women. Most of the houses not burned were robbed. . . . So many had been killed that every man we met on the street seemed to come from the dead. The first salutation was: "Why, are you alive?" The embers were still red, the fires were still burning, as we began to gather the dead and wounded from among the ruins.

★ *Gideon Welles* ★

LINCOLN'S FINAL MOMENTS

On April 14, 1865, Abraham Lincoln became yet another casualty of the war. John Wilkes Booth, a Southern actor, shot and killed Lincoln while the president was watching a play at Ford's Theater in Washington, D.C. Six Union soldiers carried the unconscious president to a boarding house across the street from the theater. Doctors there were unable to help. Lincoln's wounds were fatal. During the night and into the morning of the next day, Lincoln edged closer to death. Word of the shooting spread across the nation. Outside the boarding house, crowds nervously waited for news. Gideon Welles, who served as Lincoln's secretary of the navy, waited at the president's bedside with Lincoln's wife, Mary Lincoln. The following passages from Welles's diary provide an eyewitness account of the president's final moments before his death at 7:22 A.M.

• **Gideon Welles, *Diary of Gideon Welles*. n.p., 1911.**

The President had been carried across the street from the theatre, to the house of a Mr. Peterson. We entered by ascending a flight of steps above the basement and passing through a long hall to the rear, where the President lay extended on a bed, breathing heavily. Several surgeons were present, at least six, I should think more. Among them I was glad to observe Dr. Hall, who, however, soon left. I inquired of Dr. H., as I entered, the true condition of the President. He replied the President was dead to all intents, although he might live three hours or perhaps longer.

The giant sufferer lay extended diagonally across the bed, which was not long enough for him. He had been stripped of his clothes. His large arms, which were occasionally exposed, were of a size which one would scarce have expected from his spare appearance. His slow, full respiration lifted the clothes with each breath that he took. His features were calm and striking. I had never seen them appear to better advantage than for the first hour, perhaps, that I was there. After that, his right eye began to swell and that part of his face became discolored. . . .

The room was small and overcrowded. The surgeons and members of the Cabinet were as many as should have been in the room, but there were many more, and the hall and other rooms in the front or main house were full. One of these rooms was occupied by Mrs. Lincoln and her attendants, with Miss Harris. Mr. Dixon and Mrs. Kinney came to her about twelve o'clock.

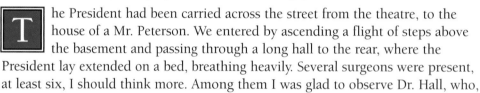

GLOSSARY

- **ascending:** climbing
- **to all intents:** for all practical purposes
- **respiration:** breathing
- **repress:** hold back, restrain
- **repair:** go
- **lamentation:** expression of grief
- **expiring:** dying
- **suspended:** stopped temporarily
- **diminish:** lessen
- **benefactor:** friend and provider

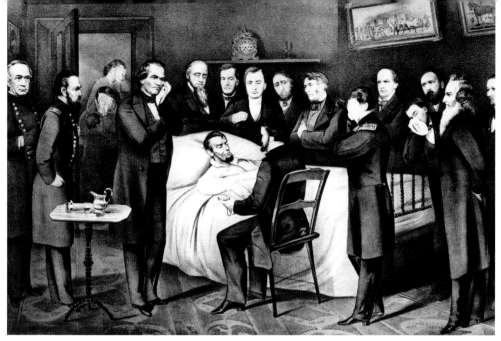

As Abraham Lincoln drew closer to death, family and prominent Union leaders came to his bedside.

About once an hour Mrs. Lincoln would repair to the bedside of her dying husband and with lamentation and tears remain until overcome by emotion.

(April 15.) A door which opened upon a porch or gallery, and also the windows, were kept open for fresh air. The night was dark, cloudy, and damp, and about six it began to rain. I remained in the room until then without sitting or leaving it, when, there being a vacant chair which some one left at the foot of the bed, I occupied it for nearly two hours, listening to the heavy groans, and witnessing the wasting life of the good and great man who was expiring before me. . . .

A little before seven, I went into the room where the dying President was rapidly drawing near the closing moments. His wife soon after made her last visit to him. The death-struggle had begun. Robert, his son, stood with several others at the head of the bed. He bore himself well, but on two occasions gave way to overpowering grief and sobbed aloud, turning his head and leaning on the shoulder of Senator [Charles] Sumner. The respiration of the President became suspended at intervals, and at last entirely ceased at twenty-two minutes past seven. . . .

I went after breakfast to the Executive Mansion. There was a cheerless cold rain and everything seemed gloomy. On the Avenue in front of the White House were several hundred colored people, mostly women and children, weeping and wailing their loss. This crowd did not appear to diminish through the whole of that cold, wet day; they seemed not to know what was to be their fate since their great benefactor was dead, and their hopeless grief affected me more than almost anything else, though strong and brave men wept when I met them.

★ *Joseph C. Rutherford* ★
DEATH TO ALL TRAITORS

Throughout the Civil War, many white Southerners insisted that their home state had a right to secede from the Union. Many Northerners, however, dismissed this argument. They viewed the rebelling Southerners as traitors. To support that view, the Northerners also pointed to the U.S. Constitution, which defines treason as waging war against the United States. Northerners who held this belief had little sympathy for Southerners when the war ended. They wanted all rebels executed or at least severely punished. Many also criticized Union officials, such as General William Tecumseh Sherman, for being too lenient when they negotiated surrender terms with Confederate leaders. Among those who favored strict punishment of Confederates was Joseph C. Rutherford, a surgeon with the Seventeenth Vermont Infantry. In an April 29, 1865, letter to his wife, Rutherford expresses his conviction that all traitors should be executed.

• **Joseph C. Rutherford, letter to Hannah Rutherford, April 29, 1865.**

My dear Wife,

I have just received your letter of the 24th and hasten to reply to it. . . . You ask my opinion of the affairs of the nation. What can *I* say—any more than I have often said—that we are coming out all right. . . .

If Sherman has done as it is said he did [negotiating lenient terms of surrender of Confederate armies in the Carolinas]—Why I think he has *dulled*—in other words made a great blunder—but so much have I become to believe in the ultimate designs of the great Ruler of all things that I feel it was intended that greater good might accrue to the nation from it. It opens the eyes of the people to the gross folly of being too lenient to these hell born traitors not only at the South but in the midst of our N.E. [New England] homes. We are all coming home soon: and our first work will be to clean out every traitor and tory—that act as foul ulcers in the living flesh of our homes. We soldiers have *vowed* it upon the altar of our country and you may depend the poisonous blood of these treacherous villians will flow freely, for the lives of many of our noble soldiers they have been the means of sacrificing. God have mercy on them for we wont—*No! Never.* . . .

You may think me excited and so I am but it is an excitement that nothing but the just punishment of traitors will allay. The country will never be safe while they are allowed to walk its surface or breathe the air of heaven—Death to all traitors is our watch word.

GLOSSARY

- **dulled:** lost his wits
- **Ruler:** God
- **accrue:** result
- **gross folly:** total foolishness
- **tory:** opponent of the Republican Party, the political party that supported the Union
- **vowed:** sworn
- **treacherous:** disloyal
- **allay:** lessen

FOR FURTHER READING

Books

Timothy Levi Biel, *Life in the North During the Civil War.* San Diego, CA: Lucent Books, 1997. A highly illustrated and informative book that examines the racial, political, and economic conditions of both the urban and rural regions of the North during the Civil War.

Stephen Currie, *The* Liberator, *Voice of the Abolitionist Movement.* San Diego, CA: Lucent Books, 2000. An informative look at the life of Northerner William Lloyd Garrison and the huge impact that his antiabolition publication *The Liberator* made on American politics and the outbreak of the Civil War.

Mary Hull, *The Union and the Civil War in American History.* Berkeley Heights, NJ: Enslow, 2000. A comprehensive look at the contributions to the Civil War by Northern soldiers, antislavery activists, U.S. government officials, and other civilians, including women and children of the North.

Russell Roberts, *Lincoln and the Abolition of Slavery.* San Diego, CA: Lucent Books, 2000. This interesting book profiles the life of Abraham Lincoln and his involvement in the slavery issue.

James Tackach, Uncle Tom's Cabin, *Indictment of Slavery.* San Diego, CA: Lucent Books, 2000. A readable, illustrated study of the impact of Harriet Beecher Stowe's antislavery novel on the people of the North and how it helped cause the American Civil War.

Websites

The American Civil War Homepage
http://sunsite.utk.edu/civil-war The largest online directory of Civil War resources, maintained by Dr. George H. Hoemann of the University of Tennessee. Includes biographical information on Union generals.

The Civil War Home Page
www.civil-war.net A database of Civil War history, with detailed information on specific battles and campaigns.

INDEX